LARGE PRINT

Other collections by Gene Ambaum & Bill Barnes:

- Unshelved
- What Would Dewey Do?
- Library Mascot Cage Match
- Book Club
- Read Responsibly
- Frequently Asked Questions
- Reader's Advisory

LARGE PRINT

an UNSHELVED® collection
by Gene Ambaum & Bill Barnes

OVERDUE MEDIA
Seattle

Reprinting *Unshelved* comic strips originally published on the *Unshelved* website from February 16, 2009 to April 26, 2010, and *ALA CogNotes* newspapers in June 2009 and January 2010.

ISBN-13: 978-0-9740353-7-6

First printing: July 2010

Printed in Canada.

FOREWORD

I'm sure many would argue that libraries are, in fact, sacred. Lush oases of knowledge in a sea of ignorance boiling over with reality TV, Hollywood scandal blogs, and Glenn Beck. And while it's true that libraries are now and will forever be on the front lines of preserving the written word, if you think the people who work there are anything close to sacred, you must be new to *Unshelved*.

I'm not going to lie to you fine people; when Bill Barnes approached me in 2009 to work with him on his second comic project, *Not Invented Here*, I had only a passing familiarity with *Unshelved*. It's just not in my wheelhouse. I already knew all I needed to know about libraries: **free books**. Like churches, libraries utilized silence and used books to make me feel guilty.

And I knew even less about the people who worked there. Even into early adulthood I was under the impression that librarians were a mysterious race of Book Elves, an evolutionary curiosity driven by some strange chromosome mutation to shush obnoxious teens, hang bifocals around their necks and wear their hair in tightly-wound buns. I even remember thinking that librarians were not employees, but rather unpaid volunteers. I'll pause here to allow the audience to snort derisively... done? Nope, few more in the back...

All right, I'll continue.

Well, that all changed when Bill sent me home one day with a complete *Unshelved* collection. That was the day my carefully-constructed illusions about librarians came crashing down around my head like an unbalanced book cart. I've had many jobs where I dealt with the public, and as I plowed through these tomes I realized that working in a library was no different. Sometimes we **hated** the public. They were ignorant and often rude. Worse, I realized that when I walk into my local library without knowing how to use the copier, put books back where they don't belong, and hog the computer, the people behind the desk do not regard me with the patience of saints. They are at work, and I make their jobs harder. (I also learned that librarians do not reproduce asexually or hang upside down from the rafters during summer vacation, but that is not germane to this conversation.)

So thanks, Bill and Gene. Not only have you given me another webcomic to add to my already-long reading list, you've also destroyed my innocence with your startling expose on the library system. I hope you're prepared to put in a good word for me. I need to return this stack of books sitting here on my coffee table...

Because they're late, and now I know I'm being judged.

PAUL SOUTHWORTH *is the co-creator, with Bill Barnes, of* Not Invented Here *(see page 68). Previously he wrote and drew* Ugly Hill. *He lives in East Providence, RI (see page 25).*

DO YOU HAVE A SCANNER I CAN USE?
NO.

IT'S NOT LIKE THEY'RE PARTICULARLY EXPENSIVE.
IT'S NOT A BUDGET PROBLEM.

THEN WHY--?
I'M REJECTING YOUR REQUEST FOR A CD PLAYER. THE LIBRARY CAN'T COMMIT TO UNPROVEN TECHNOLOGY.

YOU DIDN'T HAVE A SCANNER SO I BOUGHT YOU ONE!
THANKS.

NOW YOU HAVE A SCANNER I CAN USE!
NO, I'M AFRAID WE DON'T.

IT'S RIGHT NEXT TO THE COMPUTER!
SO NEAR AND YET SO FAR.

JUST HOOK UP THIS SCANNER SO I CAN USE IT!
IT'S NOT THAT SIMPLE.

YES IT IS! IT COMES WITH CABLES AND SOFTWARE!
ALL OUR COMPUTERS ARE LOCKED DOWN TO PROTECT THEM FROM PEOPLE LIKE YOU.

YOU CAN'T HELP ME, CAN YOU?
I'VE TOLD YOU THAT A FEW TIMES ALREADY.
BB

LARGE PRINT

WHAT'S THAT SMELL?
DEFENSE MECHANISM. IT'S HOW THE NETWORK WARDS OFF PREDATORS.

WHY DID THE SCREEN GO BLANK?
IT WON'T LET ME TYPE!
ALL MY FILES WERE DELETED!
IT SAID "PLUG AND PLAY".
WELL I'VE GOT A HIGH SCORE BREWING HERE.
BB

ON THE ONE HAND YOU CLEARLY VIOLATED LIBRARY POLICY.

ON THE OTHER HAND, YOU WENT THE EXTRA MILE IN THE NAME OF CUSTOMER SERVICE.

PLUS HE BROUGHT DOWN THE ENTIRE NETWORK!
TOO LATE, SHE'S OUT OF HANDS!

UNSHELVED®

This strip prompted a complaint from a company that sells books both on tape and on CD.

LARGE PRINT

I SIMPLY DON'T THINK THIS BELONGS IN A LIBRARY.
THIS *TOTALLY* BELONGS IN A LIBRARY.

WHAT IDIOT BOUGHT THIS?
I DID.

I CAN SEE I'M NOT MAKING MUCH HEADWAY.
DON'T GET DISCOURAGED. YOU'RE MUCH MORE LINEAR THAN MOST OF OUR CRACKPOTS.
BB

WHAT AM I SUPPOSED TO *DO* ABOUT GETTING *RID* OF THIS *BOOK*?
HOW ABOUT TAKING THE CIVILIZED ROUTE AND WRITING A LETTER?

WOULD THAT *HELP*?
NO, BUT YOU'D BE WASTING YOUR TIME POLITELY AND WITH A CERTAIN CLASSIC CHARM.
BB

SOON YOU'LL GET A FORM LETTER EXPLAINING WHY YOU WERE WRONG ABOUT THAT BOOK YOU HATE.

IT'S WRITTEN REALLY WELL. YOU'LL COME TO FEEL THAT YOU WERE PART OF A CRUCIAL REVIEW PROCESS.

I DON'T THINK I WANT TO BE MANIPULATED TO THAT DEGREE.
THEN I RECOMMEND STARTING ALL OVER AGAIN.
HERE, I NEVER LIKED THIS ONE.
BB

The 2009 recession had the effect of making libraries *the* place to be. Because, you know, they're free.

LARGE PRINT

If you don't know what Dewey is talking about in panel one, you're not alone. DC comics keeps publishing increasingly confusing "Crisis" mega-crossovers.

I NEED HELP WITH TWEETING.
BIRDCALLS, AISLE FIVE.

I'M TALKING ABOUT *TWITTER*.
YOU'RE NOT MAKING ANY SENSE. THIS MUST BE ABOUT THE INTERNET.

I WANT ***FOLLOWERS***!
TRY WALKING OUT THE DOOR. WITH LUCK SOMEONE WILL GO WITH YOU.
BB

I'VE BEEN ON *TWITTER* FOR A ***YEAR*** AND THE ONLY PERSON WHO READS ME IS MY ***MOM***!
A CULT OF PERSONALITY REQUIRES PERSONALITY.
BB

WHAT ***IS*** "*TWITTER*"?
MICROBLOGGING.

MUST YOU DEFINE GOBBLEDEGOOK WITH ***MORE*** GOBBLEDEGOOK?
SHORT, FREQUENT NOTES, AS OPPOSED TO OCCASIONAL LONGER POSTS.
BB

IS THAT ***MORE*** WORK OR ***LESS***?
IT'S MORE ***IMMEDIATE***.
IS THAT ***MORE*** WORK OR ***LESS***?

LARGE PRINT

largelibrarian I don't get Twitter.
6 minutes ago from web

deweymls @largelibrarian Just say what's on your mind.
5 minutes ago from web

largelibrarian Some people have really bad breath.
4 minutes ago from web

deweymls @largelibrarian Good! Now try to focus more on your current experience.
3 minutes ago from web

largelibrarian @deweymls I am.
2 minutes ago from web

deweymls @largelibrarian Don't worry, eventually you'll pick up the nuances.
1 minute ago from web

YOUNG MAN, WHY AREN'T YOU AT SCHOOL?
I AM.

ARE YOU SASSING ME?
I DON'T THINK SO, BUT I'LL GET A DICTIONARY SO I CAN BE SURE.

I'M CALLING THE TRUANCY OFFICER!
THEN YOU'LL HAVE TO DIAL 1957, BECAUSE I DON'T THINK THEY HAVE THOSE ANYMORE.

WHAT ARE YOU DOING ABOUT THE JUVENILE DELINQUENT?
WHICH ONE?

HIM! HE SHOULD BE IN SCHOOL!
OH, SANJAY IS HOMESCHOOLED.

BUT... HE'S NOT HOME!
NEITHER ARE YOU, BUT I'M NOT COMPLAINING.
WELL, NOT TO YOUR FACE, ANYWAY.

IS THAT HER?
SHE WOULDN'T BELIEVE I WAS HOMESCHOOLED.

WHY DIDN'T YOU SHOW HER YOUR HOMESCHOOL I.D.?
NO SUCH THING.

PLEASE DON'T GET ME IN TROUBLE.
AGAIN.

That's Bill's (homeschooling) wife in the last panel.

I'VE GOT NOTHING TO DO.
YOU MIGHT LEARN SOMETHING BY JOINING A WORK-RELATED **LISTSERV** OR **MESSAGE BOARD**!
I THINK I EXPERIENCE ENOUGH CONFLICT.
YOU PUT **MUSTARD** ON MY **SANDWICH**!
YOU WEREN'T SUPPOSED TO **EAT** THAT UNTIL YOU WERE AT **WORK**!
BB

LOOK! A WORK-RELATED PERIODICAL!
SO IT IS.

YOU'RE NOT MOVING TO PICK IT UP.
BE SATISFIED THAT I'M NOT **FLEEING**.

THIS BEHAVIOR IS UNACCEPTABLE.
YOU MEAN "LACK OF BEHAVIOR."

GO OUT IN THE **STACKS**! SEEK OUT A **PATRON**!
I'VE SOUGHT. NO ONE NEEDS HELP.

THEN DO SOMETHING IN **BACK**!
AND **ABANDON** MY **POST**?

LARGE PRINT

WE'RE JUST NOT GIVEN ENOUGH TIME TO THINK AS PROFESSIONALS. PEOPLE AND PAPERWORK GET IN THE WAY.

SO I THOUGHT I'D JUST SIT HERE AND TRY TO FIGURE THINGS OUT WHILE I HAD A FREE MINUTE.
AND YOU KNOW WHAT? I HAD A GREAT IDEA!

LET ME HEAR IT!
NOW YOU MADE ME FORGET IT.

YOU LOOK BORED.
IT'S NOT JUST A LOOK.

YOU NEED SOME FRESH AIR! OR A VITAMIN SUPPLEMENT!
I NEED SOMEONE TO ASK ME A QUESTION.

DO... DO YOU HAVE A QUESTION?
SORRY, JUST HACKNEYED ADVICE.
EXERCISE!
FLOSS!

I'VE FOUND AN ONLINE CIRCLE OF LIKE-MINDED LIBRARIANS TO COMPLAIN WITH!
WHAT IS THERE TO COMPLAIN ABOUT ON A DAY LIKE THIS?
YOUR COPY MACHINE WON'T LET ME UPLOAD MY FOLLICLES TO THE WAR ZONE!
BB

DO YOU KNOW WHAT I LOVE ABOUT MY JOB?
THE EXECUTIVE PERKS AND FRINGE BENEFITS?

HUH?
NOTHING. WHAT DO YOU LOVE ABOUT YOUR JOB?

PEOPLE REALLY APPRECIATE US!
WHICH ONE OF YOU TURNED MY SON INTO A SOCIALIST?

HOW ARE YOU TODAY?
NOT HAPPY WITH ANY OF YOU!

LET'S SEE IF WE CAN CHANGE THAT!
I WON'T FALL FOR ANY OF YOUR LIBERAL BRAINWASHING.

THIS IS NOT THE LIBRARIAN YOU'RE LOOKING FOR.
I'LL GO GET YOU A COOKIE!

YOU EXPOSED MY SON TO DANGEROUS IDEAS!
THAT'S PRETTY MUCH MY JOB DESCRIPTION.
BB

LARGE PRINT

I DON'T HAVE TIME TO MONITOR MY SON EVERY SECOND!
THAT'S FUNNY, NEITHER DO WE.
BB

YOU TURNED MY SON AGAINST ME!
HE'S A TEENAGER. THE ODDS WERE NEVER IN YOUR FAVOR.
BB

WHAT DID YOU DO TODAY?
DEALT WITH AN UPSET PARENT. AS YOU WELL KNOW.

WHY WOULD YOU THINK I KNEW THAT?
FROM THE WAY YOU NEVER LEFT YOUR OFFICE.

I WAS DOING PAPERWORK!
YOU WERE DOING PAPERWORK S-L-O-W-L-Y.
BB

YOUR SOCKS HAVE ANIMALS ON THEM.
YES!

WHAT ARE YOU, SIX YEARS OLD?
INSIDE!

WHAT DOES IT TAKE TO GET UNDER HER SKIN?
MORE THAN YOU'VE GOT.
BB

NO ONE'S REALLY THAT HAPPY.

YOU'RE WORKING AT A DESK. IN A LIBRARY.

YOU'RE A LIBRARIAN, FOR GOD'S SAKE!
EXACTLY! HOW COULD I BE HAPPIER?
BB

YOU CAN'T THROW ME OUT FOR BUGGING HER!
SHE'S WAVING AT ME!
WAVING IS HER WAY OF ASKING ME TO GET YOU OUT OF HERE.
BUT SHE'S STILL SMILING!
I INTERPRET THAT AS APPROVAL FOR YOUR IMMINENT DEPARTURE.
BB

SAFETY IS OUR NEW PRIORITY.
I THOUGHT SERVING OUR PATRONS WAS OUR PRIORITY.
SAFETY FIRST!

IT IS.
THEN ISN'T IT "SAFETY SECOND"?
I BELIEVE THAT CHILDREN ARE OUR FUTURE!
WHAT ABOUT BOOKS? AREN'T THEY A PRIORITY?
SAFETY
PRETTY IMPORTANT!

WHY AREN'T YOU AT THE DESK?
SAFETY
PRETTY IMPORTANT!
I MIGHT TRIP ON THE WAY THERE.

LIBRARY TIP #56: TAKE IT UP WITH THE MANAGER
GET ME THE MANAGER!
SHE HATES COMPLAINTS.
SHE'LL GET BACK AT US BY SCHEDULING MY SHIFTS WHEN YOU'RE MOST LIKELY TO COME IN.
AND NEITHER OF US WANTS THAT.
IT'S SO QUIET TODAY!
LET'S KEEP IT THAT WAY.

A VENDING MACHINE? IS THIS A TRUCK STOP OR A LIBRARY?
ARE THOSE OUR ONLY CHOICES?
BB

WHAT ABOUT "INTERNET CAFE"?
"PUBLIC RESTROOM"
"DAYCARE"
A VENDING MACHINE?
S'MORE?

OUR VENDING MACHINES LEAD TO NONRECYCLABLE WASTE!
SHE MEANS "GARBAGE".
READI

THEY'RE MISSING MY FAVORITE SNACK!
HE MEANS "VENISON JERKY".
READI

THEY'RE HERE TO STAY.
SHE MEANS "THEY'LL BE GONE BY END OF WEEK."
WHAT, TOO SOON?
READI

YOUR VENDING MACHINE ATE MY MONEY! I WANT A REFUND!
I'M NOT AUTHORIZED TO DO THAT.

WHAT ARE YOU AUTHORIZED TO DO?
I COULD WAIVE YOUR FINES.

I DON'T HAVE ANY FINES.
THEN I CAN OFFER YOU TOILET PAPER.
OR TONER.

YOU GOT PEANUT BRITTLE ON MY COMPUTER!
YOU GOT COMPUTER ON MY PEANUT BRITTLE!

YOU'RE SUPPOSED TO SUGGEST THAT WE'RE BETTER TOGETHER!
YOU'RE SUPPOSED TO CLOSE YOUR MOUTH WHEN CHEWING.
BB

LIBRARY TIP #57: USE THE LIBRARY FROM THE COMFORT OF HOME
I EMAILED YOU A REFERENCE QUESTION.
WE'LL RESPOND WITHIN 24 HOURS.
IT SAID RESPONSES WOULD BE "PROMPT".
NEXT DAY IS PROMPT.
I CHANGED MY MIND. I WANT TO ASK IN PERSON.
SORRY, NO DOUBLE BOOKING.

"WHAT DO YOU WORRY MOST ABOUT?"
ARE THE BOOKS IN ORDER?
STAFFING THE LIBRARY DURING A RECESSION.
WILL MY DAUGHTER GET INTO A GOOD LIBRARY SCHOOL?
DARK CITY OR PRINCE OF DARKNESS?
BB

This sequence is inspired by Gene, who is constantly pricing things he has no intention of buying.

This is the home of our friend Paul Southworth, who wrote the foreword to this book. At the time this book went to press it was still for sale, if you're interested.

HEY, I READ THAT!

THAT'S THE ONLY NOVEL MY MOTHER AND I AGREE ON!

WHAT HAPPENED TO YOUR BOOK?
TOO POPULAR.

I'M SUPPOSED TO DO BOOK REPAIRS.
IT'S NOT REPAIR. IT'S CAMOUFLAGE.

AWESOME! WHAT KIND? JUNGLE? DESERT?
NAUSEATING!
BATH OF BLOOD

I DON'T THINK THAT'S AN OPTION.
EEEEEEEEK!
BB

THAT'S DISGUSTING!
DON'T JUDGE A BOOK BY ITS COVER.
BB

I'M NOT. I'M JUDGING YOU BY ITS COVER.
I'M STANDING UP FOR MY RIGHT TO READ WHATEVER I WANT.

AND I'M STANDING UP AND WALKING AWAY.
I KNEW THE LIMBS FLOATING IN THE BLOOD WOULD PUSH YOU OVER THE EDGE.

LARGE PRINT

WHAT ARE YOU READING NOW?
SOMETHING I FOUND IN THE LIBRARY!

BUT THAT... THAT'S **AWFUL**!
LET ME READ THE BEST PART TO YOU!

WHAT'S THE **BEST** PART?
THE SON'S TEARFUL REUNION WITH HIS DAD.
NOT THAT **SHE'LL** EVER KNOW.

CONGRATULATIONS. YOU EMPTIED OUT THE ENTIRE CAFE WITH THAT **AWFUL** BOOK COVER YOU MADE.
WHEN YOU'RE AN **INTELLECTUAL FREEDOM FIGHTER** YOU LEARN TO ACCEPT COLLATERAL DAMAGE.
BB

YOU'RE **RE**-RECOVERING THAT BOOK?
MISSION ACCOMPLISHED!

WOW! WHAT WAS THE MISSION?
TO GET PEOPLE TO LEAVE ME ALONE WHEN I READ.
RE

I'LL NEVER REALLY UNDERSTAND YOUR JOB.
WELL I DO HAVE A MASTER'S DEGREE.
BB

I NEED HELP WITH MY RESUME.

I'M LOOKING FOR TIPS ON MAKING IT MORE *PRESENTABLE*.

SHARPEN YOUR CRAYON.
DO YOU THINK HOT MAGENTA WAS A GOOD CHOICE?
BB

I FORGOT MY GLASSES. WILL YOU FILL OUT THIS JOB APPLICATION FOR ME?

"REASON FOR LEAVING PREVIOUS POSITION?"
HOMICIDAL RAGE.

EXCUSE ME?
WENT AFTER A CO-WORKER WITH A SPORK.
TOO MUCH DETAIL?

I'M LOOKING FOR *JOBS*.
BUT NOT THE ONES EVERYONE *ELSE* HEARS ABOUT.

NOT IN THE *PAPER*.
NOT ON THE *INTERNET*.
NOT ON *JOBLINES*.
NO *WORD OF MOUTH*.
YOU KNOW, THE *OTHER* ONES.
THE *GOOD* ONES.

I'LL JUST GO GET THAT FILE OUT OF THE VAULT.
BE QUICK, I PARKED IN FRONT OF A HYDRANT.
BB

LARGE PRINT

THANKS TO THE RECESSION WE'RE SPENDING MORE TIME HELPING WITH JOB SEARCHES.

SO I BOUGHT THIS RESUME SOFTWARE. IT AUTOMATES EVERYTHING!
RESUME
REVENGE

YOU'RE SKEPTICAL.
HOW CAN YOU TELL?
YOU'RE AWAKE.
BB

I CAN'T FIGURE OUT THIS RESUME SOFTWARE.
"TYPE YOUR NAME" SEEMS PRETTY INTUITIVE...

I THOUGHT SO TOO.
WAIT, WHY DID IT REJECT THAT?

"DON'T NOT CLICK NOW"?
PEOPLE DON'T HAVE UPC CODES!
I FEEL VALIDATED. BUT I STILL NEED A RESUME.
BB

WHY AREN'T YOU DIRECTING PEOPLE TO THE NEW RESUME SOFTWARE?
BECAUSE I VALUE MY TIME.
AND SANITY.

BUT IT DOESN'T REQUIRE ANY STAFF TIME!
IN THEORY.

THERE'S NO DIFFERENCE BETWEEN THEORY AND PRACTICE!
THAT'S YOUR EPITAPH RIGHT THERE.
BB

WHAT ARE YOU LISTENING TO?
THE NEW U2 ALBUM. IT'S EXCELLENT!

WHO'S "U2"?
WHAT'S AN "ALBUM"?

I THINK HE BOUGHT IT.
HE'S GOT MONEY AND POWER, BUT AGE IS THE GREAT EQUALIZER.

THIS BOOK IS NOT "NEW".
IT'S SLIGHTLY USED, BUT PERFECTLY SERVICEABLE.

IT WAS ON YOUR "NEW BOOKS" SHELF.
THOSE ARE NEW TO THE LIBRARY.

THEN YOU NEED MORE PRECISE LABELS!
LIKE MANY ORGANIZATIONS, WE FIND THAT IMPRECISION MAKES FOR BETTER MARKETING.

I'M HOPING YOU'RE THE BEST LIBRARIAN HERE.
IT'S LUNCH. I'M THE ONLY LIBRARIAN HERE.

THEN I GUESS YOU'RE THE BEST.
ALSO THE WORST.

AND THE TALLEST! AND THE SHORTEST!
AND THE OLDEST! AND THE YOUNGEST!
WAS THERE AN ACTUAL QUESTION?
BB

LARGE PRINT

IT'S OKAY.
IT'S OKAY ASSUMING YOUR ALLOWANCE WILL PAY TO REPLACE THAT BOOK.

THAT'S NOT THE MOST HELPFUL THING YOU COULD SAY.
WHAT WOULD HELP MORE?

DISPLAY GENEROSITY OF SPIRIT!
I'LL INCLUDE PAPER TOWELS WITH A LIST OF YOUR FINES.

THIS IS UNCLEAN.
OKAY.

NO IT'S NOT OKAY. IT'S *FILTHY*!
THE LIBRARY SERVES A WIDE VARIETY OF PATRONS.

THERE IS ACTUAL **DIRT** ON THIS BOOK!
OH HEY, YEAH, THAT THING'S A MESS.
BB

AFTER YOU HANDLE THE BOOK, WASH YOUR HANDS WITH SOAP AND WATER.

MAKE SURE YOU LATHER FOR AT LEAST THIRTY SECONDS.

ANY OTHER ADVICE?
AVOID MEAT. IT'S FULL OF GERMS AND BAD KARMA.
MUST HELPFULNESS ALWAYS TURN TO PROPAGANDA?
BB

SORRY, HONEY, I CAN'T READ THAT TO YOU RIGHT NOW.
THEN I GUESS *I'LL* DO IT.

YOU DON'T SEEM TOO *HAPPY* ABOUT IT.
I'VE GOT PLACES TO BE. BUT I PROMISED HER A STORY.

LET'S GET THIS OVER WITH.
ON SECOND THOUGHT, I *DO* HAVE TIME.

LIBRARY TIP #58: JUDGE A BOOK BY ITS COVER
THIS DOESN'T LOOK GOOD.
IT'S NOT.
YOU *READ* IT?
OF COURSE NOT.
ANY SUGGESTIONS?
RESHELVE IT AND BACK AWAY SLOWLY.

LIBRARY TIP #59: YOU CAN'T TEACH AN OLD COMPUTER NEW TRICKS
I'M GOING TO EDIT SOME VIDEO.
NOT ON *THAT* RELIC.
WHERE CAN I FIND SOMETHING NEWER?
COMPUTER STORE.
WILL THIS AT LEAST DO RED EYE?
ONLY IF YOU STARE AT IT LONG ENOUGH.
BB

READY?
I WAS *BORN* READY.
AFTER THAT EVERYTHING WENT DOWNHILL.
BB

JURY DUTY!
I FEEL LIKE I WON THE ANTI-LOTTERY.

YOU GET TO DO YOUR CIVIC DUTY!
I WONDER HOW MUCH COFFEE I CAN BRING INTO A COURTROOM.

YOU WANT TO BE ALERT TO ENSURE JUSTICE IS DONE!
I WANT TO AVOID BEING THROWN INTO JAIL FOR NAPPING.
I'M THINKING HYDRATION PACK.
PLUS A HIP FLASK FOR EMERGENCIES.
BB

YOU DON'T KNOW HOW LUCKY YOU ARE!
YOU'VE NEVER GOTTEN JURY DUTY?

EVERY YEAR.
AND EVERY YEAR I TELL THE JUDGE I LOVE EVERYBODY EQUALLY.
AND EVERY YEAR SHE EXCUSES ME AGAINST MY WILL.
BB

I WONDER IF THAT WOULD WORK FOR ME!
PROBABLY NOT. YOU'LL BE UNDER OATH.

I'M REPORTING FOR JURY DUTY.
MALLVILL
COURTHOU
AND
DRIVE-THRO
PET SHAMP

I'LL ALERT THE MEDIA.

ALL THE ELECTRICAL OUTLETS ARE TAKEN, THE COMFORTABLE CHAIRS ARE OCCUPIED, AND THE COFFEE MACHINE IS BROKEN.
I FEEL STRANGELY AT HOME HERE.
BB

JUROR 18, YOU'RE A *LIBRARIAN*?
NO, I THOUGHT IT WAS A GOOD IDEA TO LIE UNDER OATH.

SO YOU'RE *NOT* A LIBRARIAN?
NO, I AM. JUST INJECTING A LITTLE LEVITY.

YOU *ANSWER QUESTIONS* ALL DAY FOR A LIVING?
YES.

THEN WHY ARE YOU SO *BAD* AT IT?
FINALLY, SOME *IRONY*.

YOU'RE BACK FROM JURY DUTY *ALREADY*?
ONLY TO TELL YOU I'LL BE SEQUESTERED FOR A *LENGTHY* TRIAL. I MAY NOT RETURN TO WORK FOR SEVERAL *WEEKS*.
BB

THEY KICKED YOU OUT, HUH?
I SET A NEW RECORD.

I GUESS THEY DON'T LIKE "FUNNY".
THAT'S HARD TO IMAGINE.

THE SHIFT KEY IS *STICKING*.
THERE ARE TWO.
BUT I CAN ONLY TYPE HALF AS FAST!
GUINNESS WILL BE *SO* DISAPPOINTED.
BB

DO YOU HAVE A LUMBAR CUSHION?
NO.

WHAT CAN YOU OFFER ME?
A WOODEN CHAIR WITH A MISSING LEG, OR A STAINED STOOL OF QUESTIONABLE ORIGIN.

HOW WOULD THOSE HELP MY BACK?
I'M JUST TRYING TO GET YOU OFF MINE.
BB

I'VE GOT ALL THE INFORMATION YOU NEED RIGHT **HERE**.

I'D BAN **YOUR** BOOKS.

YOU CAN VOLUNTEER AT **MY** LIBRARY ANY TIME!

WHAT DO YOU **DO** AT HARRASSMENT TRAININGS, ANYWAY?
HIT ON MY CLASSMATES.
THEY'RE BORED AND THEY'RE NOT ALLOWED TO LEAVE.
BB

IS THAT ENOUGH PERSONAL INFORMATION?
SOME MIGHT SAY **TOO** MUCH.

I WANTED TO ENSURE YOU HAD EVERYTHING YOU NEEDED.
YOU'RE JUST GETTING A **LIBRARY CARD**.

SO THE PART ABOUT MY NIGHT SWEATS WAS...?
... SOMETHING I'M TRYING HARD TO FORGET.
BB

LIBRARY TIP #61: JUST SAY "NO"

I NEED A NEW CAREER.
WE HAVE LOTS OF RESOURCES THAT CAN HELP YOU!

THERE ARE BOOKS, DATABASES THAT OFFER CAREER GUIDANCE, AND SOME GREAT WEBSITES.
BUT MY FIRST RECOMMENDATION IS ACTUALLY A LOCAL AGENCY THAT HELPS PEOPLE JUST LIKE *YOU!*
IS THERE A PROBLEM?
THAT'S WHERE I WORK.
BB

I'M LOOKING FOR A RECESSION PROOF CAREER.
THAT'S A TOUGH ONE.

YOU'RE STILL WORKING. I WANT A JOB LIKE *YOURS!*

YOU *WANT* TO BE OVEREDUCATED, UNDERPAID, AND UNDERAPPRECIATED?
SO LONG AS I DON'T HAVE TO DRESS LIKE *YOU*, SURE.
BB

YOU HAVE UNREALISTIC CAREER EXPECTATIONS.
BB

THERE AREN'T MANY JOBS WHERE YOU GET PAID A BUNDLE FOR NOT DOING MUCH. NO MATTER *WHAT* THE INFOMERCIALS SAY.

IT'S ABOUT *DOING* HARD WORK, NOT *AVOIDING* IT.
UNDERSTAND?
YES! I'M BUYING MORE LOTTERY TICKETS!

WE'VE BECOME NOTHING BUT A JOB-PLACEMENT SERVICE.
THAT'S FINE WITH ME!

LIBRARIES AREN'T STATIC. THEY GO WITH THE FLOW, BECOMING WHAT THE COMMUNITY NEEDS.
IN BOOM TIMES WE PROVIDED ENTERTAINMENT. NOW WE'RE A RESOURCE FOR ECONOMIC VICTIMS.
IT'S ALL ABOUT BEING OPEN-MINDED AND FLEXIBLE.
BB

I'D LIKE TO BUY MORE VIDEO GAMES AND GRAPHIC NOVELS.
OVER MY DEAD BODY.

I NEED A JOB THAT'S FUTURE-PROOF!
HOW ABOUT ONE THAT WILL LAST UNTIL THE END OF THE WEEK?
SOLD!

"WHAT'S YOUR SECRET?"
FIBER.
BB
FULLY HYDROGENATED FATS!
PEANUT FUDGE UNITS
STUDENT MAKEOVERS AT THE MALLVILLE BEAUTY ACADEMY.
THE ALPHABET.

I THOUGHT YOU ASKED FOR GRAY'S ANATOMY.
HE'S NOT SO McDREAMY WITHOUT HIS McSKIN.
BB

YOU CAN'T ANSWER QUESTIONS USING WIKIPEDIA!

THAT INFORMATION ISN'T VETTED! YOU HAVE TO USE A TRUSTWORTHY, ACCURATE SOURCE!

I SAY WE LET THE MARKET DECIDE.
YOU HAPPY?
I'M GREAT, THANKS.
BB

THAT DOESN'T LOOK FISCALLY RESPONSIBLE.
IT'S THE MIGHTY MUGGS BIGGS DARKLIGHTER FIGURE!

I'M JUMPSTARTING THE ECONOMY. AND INVESTING IN THE FUTURE.

PLUS HE LOOKED SO FORLORN UP THERE ON THE SHELF.
HE DOES HAVE PUPPYDOG EYES UNDER HIS HELMET.
BB

"LIBRARIANSHIP: IT'S NOT JUST A JOB, IT'S ...?"

I RESERVED A ROOM FOR THIS AFTERNOON.

PERFECT. THE BOUNCY CASTLE GOES THERE, AND THE BUFFET GOES THERE!
I TRUST YOU READ THE ROOM USE AGREEMENT?

SPECIFICALLY **SECTION FIVE: NO PARTIES**.
THIS WILL BE THE BEST BIRTHDAY EVER!
BB

THIS IS A PUBLIC SPACE. EVEN IF WE LET YOU HAVE YOUR DAUGHTER'S BIRTHDAY, IT WOULD HAVE TO BE OPEN TO **EVERYONE**.
WHO'D WANT TO COME TO A FIVE-YEAR OLD'S PARTY?
BB

WILL THERE BE CAKE? OR FOOD OF ANY KIND?
REMEMBER TO GET ICE CREAM. VANILLA. CAN I USE YOUR PHONE TO INVITE MY FRIENDS?
I CAN MAKE A BALLOON EMU! BUT I'LL NEED A LIVE EMU AS A MODEL.

I'M OUT OF TIME. I'LL PAY WHATEVER YOU **WANT**.
THERE'S NO CHARGE. IT'S JUST NOT **ALLOWED**.

WHAT MIGHT IT TAKE TO **IGNORE** THE RULES?
PERHAPS A GENEROUS CONTRIBUTION EARMARKED FOR TEEN PROGRAMS?

AND WHAT ABOUT THE **PUBLIC**?
A STEADY STREAM OF BIRTHDAY CAKE SHOULD KEEP THEM AT BAY.
BB

We don't know either.

True story. Gene's mom.

LARGE PRINT

I'M GLAD YOU'RE TRYING "SANE AND REASONABLE".
I WISH YOU'D GONE WITH THAT FROM THE START.
BUT I HAVE TO STRESS THAT IT STILL WOULDN'T HAVE GOTTEN YOU WHAT YOU WANT.
BB

HE WON'T HELP US!
HELP THEM.
NO.
I'LL SUE!
SHE'LL SUE!
THAT WON'T GET ANYONE TO THE CONCERT.
YOU PROMISED!
YOU PROMISED?
SHE PROMISED.

IF YOU BUY THOSE TICKETS I'LL PAY YOU DOUBLE THEIR FACE VALUE.
THIRD ROW CENTER? I'D SAY THEY'RE WORTH TRIPLE.

DONE! I'LL PA
NO! I CAN'T LET THIS HAPPEN!

AND SO MY CREDIT CARD AND I LEAVE YOU AND MY VILLAINOUS MANAGER IN OUR WAKE AS WE RIDE INTO THE SUNSET.
THIS IS YOUR FAULT!
BB

I CAN'T BELIEVE I DID THAT!
FARTED DURING STORYTIME?

WORSE! I SWORE! IT JUST CAME OUT!
I'M SURE NO ONE EVEN NOTICED.

DAGNABBIT! DAGNABBIT! DAGNABBIT!
I'M RUINED.
BB

I'M SO SORRY!
HE SOUNDS LIKE ELMER FUDD!
DAGNABBIT!

I REALLY NEED TO APOLOGIZE.
NO WORRIES.
DAG-NABID!
BB

THIS IS MY FAULT.
THEN I INSIST YOU RESIGN.
YOU REALLY DO CREATE YOUR OWN PROBLEMS.
DAD GUMMIT!

I WILL NEVER DO THAT AGAIN, I SWEAR!
NO! I DON'T SWEAR!
I MUSN'T SWEAR!
I AFFIRM!

LANGUAGE IS SO FLUID.
THAT MAKES ME HAVE TO MICTURATE.
BB

YOU CAN'T WRITE TAMARA UP.
SHE DIDN'T SWEAR.
SHE USED A CARTOON WORD!
I HAVE TO.
A PARENT COMPLAINED.
THIS HAS GONE UP THE LADDER.
I HAVE TO BEGIN DISCIPLINARY PROCEDURES!

THEN ISN'T IT IMPROPER TO DISCUSS IT WITH ME?
I... I...
I'D HATE TO SEE YOU GET WRITTEN UP TOO.
BB

I'M LOOKING FOR AN EXPERT.
I'M AFRAID I'M A GENERALIST.

DO YOU THINK YOU'LL BE ABLE TO HELP ME?
IF YOU BELIEVE IN ME, CLAP YOUR HANDS!

NOW I'M CONFUSED.
THEN WE'RE READY TO START.
BB

"HOP ON ONE LEG, PUT A THUMB TACK UNDER YOUR HEEL, OR GO SHAMPOO YOUR CAT."

WHAT WAS THAT?
THE LAST ANSWER I GAVE. I THOUGHT IT MIGHT JOG YOUR MEMORY.

I THINK I WANTED A BOOK.
WANT TO HEAR WHAT I HAD FOR LUNCH?

YOU'RE SUPPOSED TO ANSWER WHEN I'M TALKING TO YOU!
WHAT ARE YOU DOING?
SEEKING THE PEACE THAT EXISTS AT THE BOTTOM OF MY CUP.
WHAT ARE YOU DOING, GOING FOR STORY OF THE DAY?
BB

AREN'T YOU HELPING SOMEONE?
YES.
OH, YOU DIDN'T MEAN ME.
BB

MORE COFFEE?
ONE CUP WASN'T ENOUGH TO GET ME THROUGH THIS.

YOU'RE RIGHT ABOUT THAT!
YES SIR!

FORGOT WHAT WAS IRRITATING YOU?
YES.
AND IF YOU GIVE ME A CUP, I'LL STOP TRYING TO REMEMBER.
BB

I REPAIRED THIS!
NO, YOU BOUGHT IT.

WE WILL BE CLOSING IN FIVE MINU
I'VE GOT A BIG PROJECT DUE TOMORROW.

LET ME GUESS. YOU NEED BOOKS, ARTICLES, ETC.
EXACTLY.

BUT I'LL SETTLE FOR A NOTE SAYING YOU DIDN'T HAVE TIME TO HELP ME.
DON'T FORGET YOUR EMAIL AND HOME PHONE.
BB

WE'RE CLOSING.
I WANT THAT NEW BLOCKBUSTER THAT JUST CAME OUT ON DVD.

ME TOO. UNFORTUNATELY, THERE'S A SIX MONTH WAIT.

I DON'T SEE A LINE.
IT STRETCHES DOWN THE BLOCK. HEAD FOR THE END AND I'LL SEE YOU IN DECEMBER.
BB

WE'RE CLOSING.
BUT I NEED MORE TIME TO FINISH!
YOU'LL NEVER FINISH.
YOU'RE SISYPHUS AND THAT RESUME IS YOUR BOULDER.
NOW I NEED TIME TO GOOGLE THAT.

TIME TO GO, LAMBERT. WE'RE CLOSED.
I NEED MORE TIME TO CHARGE MY PHONE.

YOU'VE BEEN HERE ALL DAY!
I'VE BEEN SLEEPING ALL DAY.

IT'S GOING TO BE A LONELY NIGHT FOR YOU.
I GUESS I'LL RE-RESORT TO TALKING TO MYSELF.
BB

WHEN DO YOU CLOSE?

I SAID, WHEN DO YOU CLOSE?
BB

ANSWER ME!
WHY IS THIS DOOR LOCKED?

"HOLIDAY BLEND?"
OUR POOR INVENTORY PLANNING LAST WINTER MEANS SAVINGS FOR YOU!
SALE!

BUT ONLY IF I LIKE A FESTIVE MIX OF DRIED EGGNOG, MISTLETOE, HOLLY, PINE NEEDLES, YULE LOG, TINSEL AND WRAPPING PAPER.

AND I DON'T.
IN SIX MONTHS IT'LL MAKE GREAT STOCKING STUFFERS FOR PEOPLE YOU DON'T LIKE!
BB

EMPIRE COUNTY GOT A GRANT FOR SOMETHING CALLED "THE BIG READ".
WE CAN DO BETTER!
BIGGER READ
LOOK WHAT COMPETITIVE CITY IS DOING!
THE BIGGEST READ
BUT WE'RE THE LITTLE LIBRARY SYSTEM THAT CAN!
THE BIGGER READ
WE'RE THE LITTLE LIBRARY SYSTEM THAT SHOULD HAVE CHOSEN THE SUPERLATIVE.
BB

COMPETITIVE CITY IS TRYING TO OUTDO US.
YOU WERE TRYING TO OUTDO EMPIRE COUNTY.

THEY'RE NOT GOING TO GET AWAY WITH THIS!
WE'LL PUT GOOD BOOKS INTO THE HANDS OF PATRONS?

WHAT'S BIGGER THAN "BIGGEST"?
I'LL GET STARTED ON THE PROGRAM WE HAVE.

FREE BOOK?
WHAT DO YOU THINK I AM, STUPID?

IF I THOUGHT THAT I'D SELL YOU A LOTTERY TICKET.
I SUPPOSE YOU NEED MY BIRTHDAY, SOCIAL SECURITY NUMBER, AND THUMBPRINT.
BB

JUST A LITTLE COMMON COURTESY.
THIS DOESN'T EVEN HAVE PICTURES!

LARGE PRINT

YOU WHAT?
I WANT TO GIVE YOU A BOOK.

YES I AM A GOOD COOK!
I EVEN HAVE A LARGE PRINT EDITION.

THANK YOU, BUT I ALREADY OWN A COFFEE TABLE.
WHEN YOU FINISH, PASS IT ON TO A FRIEND!

YOU'VE REALLY GOTTEN BEHIND THIS PROGRAM.
THAT'S BECAUSE THE PRESSURE IS OFF!
ON ONE SIDE WE HAVE THE GIANT LIBRARY SYSTEM WITH FEDERAL GRANT MONEY.
ON THE OTHER, AN INNOVATIVE CITY LIBRARY DETERMINED TO OUTDO US.
EXPECTATIONS ARE LOW! I CAN BE MYSELF.
TRY IT!
FREE BOOK?
ONLY IF IT COMES WITH A HUG.
AND DINNER.

DID YOU GET THE OTHER LIBRARIES TO CEASE AND DESIST?
THEY LAUGHED AT ME.
THEY WERE RUDE.
CRUDE.
THEY CALLED ME NAMES.
YOU COULD HAVE HAD ALL THAT WITHOUT LEAVING THE BUILDING.
WOULD A FREE BOOK CHEER YOU UP?

THE PERFECT WEEK
WHEN SOMEONE WANTS A COMPUTER, ONE BECOMES AVAILABLE.
AND WHEN SOMEONE GIVES UP A COMPUTER...
SOMEONE ELSE TAKES HIS PLACE.
IT'S MAKING ME A LITTLE QUEASY.

THE PERFECT WEEK
ALL DAY LONG, EVERY BOOK I'VE LOOKED FOR HAS BEEN ON THE SHELF.
EXACTLY WHERE IT'S SUPPOSED TO BE.
DO YOU HAVE ANY BOOKS ON TUVAN COOKING?
ON ANY OTHER DAY? NO. BUT TODAY I'M SURE I CAN HELP YOU.
BB

THE PERFECT WEEK
I CAN HAVE THESE FOR FOUR WEEKS? THAT'S MORE THAN ENOUGH!
TWO HOURS OF COMPUTER TIME? SO GENEROUS!
THIS OVERDUE FINE IS REASONABLE, AND WILL DISCOURAGE ME FROM KEEPING BOOKS FOR TOO LONG.
HOW DID YOU BRAINWASH THEM?
SERIOUSLY. I'M LOOKING FOR TIPS.

THE PERFECT WEEK
WATCH THIS.
I HAVE TO ASK YOU TO...
I APOLOGIZE FOR BREAKING THE RULES!
NO PHONES
IT WILL NEVER HAPPEN AGAIN!
I'M GOING TO MY OFFICE TO SEE IF MY MONTHLY REPORTS WILL WRITE ***THEMSELVES***!
CRUNCH!
BB

THE PERFECT WEEK
NO KIDS LOOKING FOR LAST-MINUTE HOMEWORK HELP.
TEENS ***HAPPY*** TO HEAR ABOUT OUR IN-DEPTH DATABASE OFFERINGS.
THANKS FOR SPENDING MY TAX DOLLARS SO ***RESPONSIBLY***!
WAKE UP! ***WAKE UP!***
BB

THE PERFECT WEEK
I HOPE THINGS GET BACK TO NORMAL. IMAGINE IF ***EVERY*** WEEK WENT SO SMOOTHLY WE WEREN'T EVEN ***NEEDED***.
WE'D TRAVEL THE LAND, SPREADING THE GOSPEL OF LIBRARIES TO ITS EVERY CORNER!
THERE'S NOT ENOUGH COFFEE IN THE WORLD.
BB

Spoiler alert: it's a true story about gay penguins.

LARGE PRINT

I'M LOOKING FOR BESTSELLERS.
HERE.

WHAT'S THIS?
TORE UP THE CHARTS IN 1973.

I WANT A *CURRENT* BESTSELLER NOT A *FORMER* BESTSELLER.
BY THE TIME IT'S *AVAILABLE* IT'LL *BE* A FORMER BESTSELLER.

WHY DON'T YOU HAVE ENOUGH BESTSELLERS FOR *EVERYONE*?
BECAUSE THEN WE'D HAVE TEN THOUSAND COPIES OF THE LATEST VAMPIRE ROMANCE.
AND *NOTHING ELSE*.
BB

WHAT'S THE POINT OF *HAVING* A LIBRARY IF I HAVE TO *WAIT* FOR THE BOOKS I WANT?
NOT INSTANT GRATIFICATION, APPARENTLY.
CATALOG

QUITE THE HEAT WAVE!
YES. YES IT IS.

GOOD THING YOU'VE GOT--
NO! DON'T!

CLATTER CLATTER THUNK!
-- AIR CONDITIONING?
YUP. YOU JINXED IT.
BB

WE'RE ON A LIST OF BUILDINGS FOR THE PUBLIC TO TAKE REFUGE FROM THE HEAT.
BUT OUR A/C ISN'T WORKING!
MALLVILLE PUBLIC LIBRARY

WE CAN EXPECT SIGNIFICANT CROWDING.
... WHICH WILL MAKE IT EVEN HOTTER.

LET'S DO EVERYTHING WE CAN FOR THEM.
WHICH IS NOTHING.
HERE'S HOPING THEY'RE TOO LETHARGIC TO COMPLAIN.
BB

YOU NEED TO DRESS PROFESSIONALLY!
PROFESSIONALISM BEGINS WITH NOT PASSING OUT FROM THE HEAT.
BB

HOT ENOUGH FOR YOU?
THE REAL QUESTION IS, IS IT HOT ENOUGH FOR *YOU*?

BECAUSE IF NOT, I'D BE HAPPY TO GET YOU A STEAMING BEVERAGE.
OR PERHAPS A HOT STONE MASSAGE?
THIS MAGNIFYING GLASS CAN FOCUS THE SUN'S RAYS ON THE AREA OF YOUR CHOOSING.

I WAS JUST MAKING CONVERSATION.
ME TOO.
HOW'S IT GOING SO FAR?

IS THAT *ICE*?
IT IS.

CAN *I* GET SOME?
THIS IS ALREADY SPOKEN FOR.

HOW'S THAT?
SEAL ME UP. I THINK I'M GOOD FOR THE NEXT HOUR.
IRE
BB

I'M HOT.
ME TOO.

I WAS HOPING YOU'D MOCK ME INTO ACTION.
HAVEN'T GOT IT IN ME.

NOTHING'S FUNNY ABOUT A HEAT WAVE.
WHO PAYS FOR THESE SWEAT STAINS?
WE ALL DO.
BB

THE SUMMER READING PRIZES STILL HAVEN'T ARRIVED.
I'M GOING TO HIDE MY ACTION FIGURES!
I FOUND THESE UNUSED PRIZES FROM BYGONE YEARS.
THIS COUPON FOR PIZZA EXPIRED IN 1985.
IS IT TOO LATE FOR READING TO BE ITS OWN REWARD?
BB

RUBBER SNAKE?
THEY USED TO BE A POPULAR NOVELTY ITEM!

I'M HERE FOR A SUMMER READING PRIZE, NOT TO HELP YOU RELIVE YOUR CHILDHOOD.
PRIZES

SEA MONKEYS?
I DON'T KNOW WHAT THAT IS, BUT I BET IT'S NOT NEARLY AS COOL AS IT SOUNDS.
BB

I READ ALL THESE SO I COULD GET A BEADING KIT.
THERE WAS A PROBLEM WITH THE SHIPMENT.

LOOK ON THE BRIGHT SIDE. YOU'RE IN FOR A SURPRISE!
I'M NOT THE ONLY ONE, LADY.

AREN'T YOU GOING TO CHOOSE AN ITEM FROM THE BOX?
ONCE I REACH MY DAD YOU'LL BE BEGGING ME TO TAKE EVERYTHING IN THE BOX.
BB

BAD DAY?
OH NO! DOES IT **SHOW**?

IT'S NO MYSTERY. SUMMER IS OVER AND NO ONE WANTS YOUR LAME READING PRIZES.
DO I LOOK **RUFFLED**?
I LOOK **RUFFLED**, DON'T I?

THERE MIGHT BE A LITTLE SALIVA ON YOUR FACE FROM THE DAD WHO YELLED AT YOU.
I'D BETTER GET MYSELF TOGETHER. I NEED TO SELL THIS TO THE KIDS.

SUMMER READING WAS GREAT THIS YEAR!
WE'RE OUT OF MAGIC KITS.

THAT'S OKAY! I READ A GREAT BOOK!
YOU... YOU DID?

IT WAS ABOUT DIRTY TRICKS! I FILLED MY BROTHER'S SHOES WITH
STOP. I'D RATHER ENJOY THE PREVIOUS MOMENT.

I READ **ALL** THESE BOOKS!
GOOD FOR YOU.

YOU DON'T **BELIEVE** ME?
I DON'T **NOT** BELIEVE YOU.

I'LL HAVE YOU KNOW I'M A **VORACIOUS** READER!
THEN I'LL FIND MORE BOOKS FOR YOU TO CLAIM TO HAVE READ.
BB

MY WIFE ASKED ME TO PICK UP A BOOK SHE RESERVED.
SORRY, YOU'RE NOT AUTHORIZED.

SHE'LL TELL YOU IT'S OKAY.
SHE HAS TO COME HERE IN PERSON.

WOULDN'T THAT DEFEAT THE *PURPOSE*?
NO, BUT IT WOULD SUFFER A SIGNIFICANT SETBACK.
BB

MY WIFE'S FACEBOOK PAGE.
MY WIFE'S TWITTER FEED.
YOUTUBE VIDEO OF MY WIFE GIVING BIRTH TO OUR SON.
I'M REQUIRED TO PROTECT HER PRIVACY, NO MATTER HOW LITTLE SHE HAS LEFT.
BB

MY HUSBAND COULDN'T CHECK OUT THE BOOK I ORDERED?
NOT WITHOUT YOUR SAY-SO.
I'M SAYING SO.
I'LL JUST NEED TO SEE YOUR ID!
THIS IS ALL TO *PROTECT* YOU, I SWEAR!
I'M NOT THE ONE WHO NEEDS *PROTECTING* RIGHT NOW!
BB

THANKS FOR MAKING ME DRIVE BACK TO MY HOUSE TO GET MY ID!
WE CAN'T BE TOO CAREFUL THESE DAYS.

SIGN HERE TO GIVE YOUR HUSBAND ACCESS TO YOUR ACCOUNT.
AND I'LL GET ACCESS TO HIS, RIGHT?
RIGHT?

WHAT'S HE BEEN CHECKING OUT?
UNTIL HE SIGNS THIS FORM IT'S BETWEEN HIM AND THE COMPUTER.

YOU CAN'T DRINK THAT COFFEE OUT HERE!
YOU CAN'T WEAR THOSE PANTS IN PUBLIC.

THERE'S BEEN A COMPLAINT.
I THINK I GOT DECAF BY MISTAKE.
BB

LIBRARY TIP #62: BOOKS AREN'T OBSOLETE YET
THIS READING DEVICE™ HOLDS MORE BOOKS THAN YOUR ENTIRE LIBRARY!
THOSE ARE NOTHING BUT DUST COLLECTORS!
DO YOU HAVE SOMEPLACE TO CHARGE THIS?
SURE. WANT A BOOK TO READ WHILE YOU'RE WAITING?

I'M HERE TO START DIGITIZING YOUR COLLECTION!
WITH A TANNING BED?

IT'S A SCANNER. I BOUGHT IT AT A GARAGE SALE. MY WIFE TOLD ME TO GET OUT OF THE HOUSE.

I'M UNEMPLOYED.
DO TELL.
BB

WHAT'S YOUR PLAN, EXACTLY?
I'M GOING TO SCAN YOUR BOOKS AND CHARGE FOR ACCESSING THEM ON MY WEBSITE!

THAT'S QUITE THE IDEA.
WELL I HAVE A LOT OF TIME TO THINK.

IT'S ALSO COMPLETELY ILLEGAL.
INFORMATION WANTS TO BE FREE. SO I CAN SELL IT.
BB

I HEARD THAT BIG COMPANIES ARE SCANNING LIBRARY BOOKS!
OLD, RARE, ORPHANED OR OUT-OF-COPYRIGHT BOOKS.

LEAD ME TO THEM!
WE DON'T HAVE ANY.
ALL WE HAVE ARE PILES OF PAST BESTSELLERS.

CAN I SCAN *THOSE*?
NO. BUT YOU'RE WELCOME TO SHINGLE YOUR HOUSE WITH THEM.
VAMPIRES!
BB

SO IF MY SCANNER WORKED...
...WHICH IT DOESN'T...

...I COULD ONLY SCAN WHAT NO ONE WANTS TO READ...
...BOOKS IN THE PUBLIC DOMAIN...

...WHICH YOU DON'T HAVE ANYWAY. SO WHAT SHOULD I *DO*?
LET ME SHOW YOU OUR FREE DATABASE OF FISHING MAGAZINES!
BB

OH-OH HERE SHE COMES...

WATCH OUT BOYS SHE'LL CHEW YOU UP...

I SUPPOSE YOU'RE GOING TO TELL ME TO PUT ON **HEADPHONES**.
NOT SO LONG AS YOU KEEP PLAYING THE GREATEST HITS OF THE EIGHTIES!
HOW WOULD I LOOK IN A **MUSTACHE**?

I NEED A BOOK ON...

... FIRST AID, COMING UP.
BB

IT'S NOT FAIR THAT YOU GET HOLIDAYS OFF.
JUST WHEN I'M **FREE** TO USE THE LIBRARY IT'S ***CLOSED***!
YOU SHOULD BE OPEN WHEN ***I'M*** AVAILABLE.

WHO ARE YOU CALLING?
IS THIS THE OBSERVATORY? EXCITING NEWS. I FOUND THE CENTER OF THE UNIVERSE!
BB

OF ***COURSE*** WE'RE HERE TO ACCOMMODATE YOU.
WHAT SHOULD WE BE DOING ***DIFFERENTLY***?

WELL... YOU CLOSE TOO EARLY.
BE MORE SPECIFIC.
BB

CAN YOU STAY OPEN UNTIL 8? OR 9?
DON'T ***ASK*** ME. ***TELL*** ME.

MONDAYS 6PM - 7PM. FRIDAYS 10PM - 11PM. NEXT THURSDAY AT 4:18PM FOR A FEW MINUTES.
AND YOU'LL LET ME KNOW ABOUT THE WEEK AFTER THAT.

IT WILL BE INCONVENIENT, BUT I'M GOING TO TELL MY BOSS TO COMPLETELY REWORK MY SCHEDULE AROUND YOURS.

THAT'S CRAZY. WHAT ABOUT ALL OF THESE ***OTHER*** PEOPLE?
THEY CALL THAT A ***MOMENT OF CLARITY.***
BB

LARGE PRINT

I FOUND THIS ON THE PRINTER.
WHAT IS IT?
BB

FOR ALL WE KNOW, CLASSIFIED INFORMATION.
THEN HAND IT OVER.

WHAT'S IT WORTH TO YOU?
NOT EVEN THE TIME THIS CONVERSATION HAS TAKEN.

I DIDN'T PRINT THAT.
SOMEONE DID. IT MAY CONTAIN THEIR DEEPEST DARKEST SECRETS.

HAVEN'T YOU LOOKED AT IT?
I'M OFFERING YOU EXCLUSIVE RIGHTS.

I'M NOT FALLING FOR *THAT* ONE AGAIN.
HOW ABOUT **SUPER**-EXCLUSIVE RIGHTS?
SOLD!

SOMEONE FOUND IT ON THE PRINTER.
LEAVE IT AT THE FRONT DESK FOR THEM TO CLAIM.
BUT DON'T LOOK AT IT - IT MIGHT BE ***PRIVATE***.

I'M LOOKING FOR A PRINTOUT I MADE.
CAN YOU DESCRIBE IT?
IT'S A ***PRINTOUT***.
THIS IS YOUR LUCKY DAY!
BB

This sequence was drawn by Paul Southworth and introduces Owen and Desmond, the main characters of Paul and Bill's comic strip *Not Invented Here*.

LARGE PRINT

WHAT DO YOU DO FOR A LIVING?
I WRITE SOFTWARE.

MANY PROGRAMMERS ENJOY THE WORKS OF NEAL STEPHENSON.
ARE THERE ANY...?
SNOW CRASH

THERE'S A GIRL WHO RIDES A SKATEBOARD BY HARPOONING MINIVANS.
HMM. PROMISING!
SNOW CRASH

THANKS FOR HELPING DESMOND FIND A BOOK.
WHAT ABOUT YOU?

OH NO, NO, I'M GOOD. ALWAYS FILLING UP THE OLD NOGGIN WITH PREMIUM UNLEADED. HALFWAY THROUGH PROUST'S LATEST!

THIS ONE HAS FUNNY PICTURES.
HA! HE HATES MONDAYS!

SO NICE TO SEE THE DIGERATI IN A BRICK BUILDING ENJOYING *PAPER BOOKS!*

THANKS! I JUST ORDERED THIS ONLINE FOR MY eBOOK READER!
SNOW CRASH

STILL, PEOPLE WILL ALWAYS NEED LIBRARIES.
WHERE'S THE BATHROOM?

I'M GOING FOR COFFEE.
NO ONE ELSE LEAVES THE BUILDING FOR COFFEE.

EVERYONE ELSE LIKES IT HERE.
WELL IT'S NOT LIKE I SLEEP IN THE REFERENCE STACKS.

... EXCEPT THAT ONE TIME.
WE'RE GOING FOR COFFEE.
BB

I CAN'T BELIEVE THIS IS YOUR FIRST TIME!
DO I LOOK LIKE SOMEONE WHO WOULD PAY $4 FOR COFFEE?
MUFFINS

WELL THEN THIS ONE'S ON ME.
I'D LIKE A DOUBLE TALL HALF-CAF SKINNY CAPPUCCINO.

I CAN'T BELIEVE THIS IS YOUR FIRST TIME!
I'M A LIBRARIAN. I DID RESEARCH.
BB

WE'RE NOT RUSHING BACK?
I USUALLY TALK BOOKS WITH THE OTHER CUSTOMERS.

BUT TODAY YOU AND I CAN TALK ABOUT THE LIBRARY!
THAT SOUNDS LIKE WORK.

DON'T YOU WANT TO HEAR ABOUT MY PLAN TO SABOTAGE THE INTERNET?
I'M IN.
BB

LARGE PRINT

LIBRARY TIP #63: SEEK HELP EARLY

I PULLED OUT MY JUMP DRIVE. BUT NOT UNTIL THE SCREEN STARTED FLASHING. WHICH WAS AFTER THE FONT TURNED INTO CHINESE. AND BEFORE, NO, *DURING* THE BUZZING.

STOP! DON'T ANSWER THAT QUESTION!

GIVE A PATRON AN ANSWER AND HE'S INFORMED FOR A DAY. SHOW HIM HOW TO FIND HIS OWN ANSWERS AND HE'S INFORMED FOR A LIFETIME!

THIS IS A TEACHABLE MOMENT!
IF YOU SAY SO.
WON'T YOU PLEASE JUST TELL ME WHERE THE BATHROOM IS?
BB

DID YOU KNOW YOU CAN USE OUR WEBSITE TO FIND THE ANSWERS TO YOUR QUESTIONS?
YOU CAN DO A FULL-TEXT SEARCH, OR ELSE TRY THE SITE INDEX.
OR TRY A COMBINED SEARCH OF ALL OF OUR DATABASES, OR OUR DIRECTORY OF WEB PAGES THAT HELP WITH HOMEWORK.
WHERE ARE YOU GOING?
BB

I JUST WANTED THE BATHROOM! WHY ARE YOU TELLING ME ABOUT EVERYTHING IN THE LIBRARY?
WELL NOT EVERYTHING. I MISSED THE CATALOG, THE REFERENCE SECTION...
WHY?
WE TELL YOU AS MUCH AS POSSIBLE WHILE WE HAVE YOUR ATTENTION.
WHY?
EVERY TIME WE TEACH SOMEONE ABOUT A RESOURCE AN ANGEL GETS ITS WINGS.
BB

This popular strip led to the even more popular t-shirt design below.

WHAT'S GOOD ABOUT JAPANESE COMICS?
MANGA ISN'T FOR EVERYONE.

MY TEENS LOVE THEM. I MEAN *LOVE* THEM.
YOU CAN'T LIKE EVERYTHING YOUR KIDS LIKE.

I NEED TO BE ABLE TO PUT ON A GOOD ACT.
I GO WITH THE TRUTH, BUT EVERYONE NEEDS A DIFFERENT SHTICK.
BB

I'M SURE WE CAN FIND A MANGA YOU'D LIKE.
PINK INK MAKES MY EYES FEEL LIKE THEY'RE BLEEDING.

I ALSO HATE BIG EYES, BIG HEADS, SWEAT, GHOSTS, FANTASY, FIGHT SCENES, SEXUAL INNUENDO ...

... BOY-BOY ROMANCES, HISTORICAL FICTION ...
I'M GOING TO GET COFFEE. THIS MIGHT BE A LONG NIGHT.
BB

THE PROBLEM ISN'T THAT YOU DON'T LIKE *MANGA*, IT'S THAT YOU DON'T LIKE *ANYTHING*.

IT'S TRUE. I DON'T EVEN LIKE *YOU*.
KEEP IN MIND THAT YOU'RE STILL WAITING FOR MY HELP.

YOU'RE LESS OBJECTIONABLE THAN MOST?
I'M HONORED.

I DIDN'T USED TO LIKE MANGA.
YOU *DIDN'T*?

I READ A DIFFERENT MANGA EVERY WEEK FOR A YEAR. EVENTUALLY I GOT USED TO THE DIFFERENCES.

WHAT ABOUT READING ***BACKWARDS***?
I ALWAYS READ THE LAST PAGE OF A BOOK FIRST, SO THAT PART WAS EASY.
BB

I'LL ***TAKE*** THESE, BUT I'M NOT GOING TO ***ENJOY*** THEM.
WITH THAT KIND OF ATTITUDE HOW CAN YOU FAIL?
BB

I WANT HER TO STOP PLAYING WITH THAT.

NOW I WANT HER TO STOP SCREAMING.

AH YES, 2PM. RIGHT ON SCHEDULE.

CUE THE MOM, FROM ACROSS THE LIBRARY.
CONSEQUENCES! THERE WILL BE CONSEQUENCES!

YOU CAN HIDE, BUT YOU CAN'T RUN.
STAY POSITIVE, TAMARA!
CONSEQUENCES!
BB

HER KIDS PULLED MY TAIL.
THEY STOMPED THE DSM-IV!
THEY'RE THRIVING! A LITTLE TOO MUCH!
SOMEONE NEEDS TO EXPLAIN THE RULES TO THAT WOMAN.
AND YET HERE WE SIT, HUDDLED LIKE PENGUINS IN A BLIZZARD.
READ
BB

I VOTE THAT DEWEY VOLUNTEERS TO TALK TO HER.
SECONDED.
SECONDED AGAIN!
I CAN'T ASSIGN TASKS BY MAJORITY VOTE!
READ
BB

I SPOKE WITH THE OTHER PATRONS AND WE ALL AGREE: DEWEY'S THE MAN FOR THE JOB.
DONE!

CONSEQUENCES!
ON BEHALF OF THE LIBRARY STAFF AND PATRONS, I'M HERE TO TELL YOU YOUR PARENTING ISN'T WORKING FOR US.

ARE YOU TALKING TO *ME*?
CONFUSING, RIGHT? WOULD IT BE EASIER IF I SHOUTED AT YOU FROM ACROSS THE ROOM?

CONSEQUENCES!
YOU'RE NOT EVEN *LOOKING* AT THEM.
I DON'T NEED TO. I KNOW MY KIDS.

YOU'LL BE *SORRY*!
NEAR-APOLOGY ACCEPTED!
BB

PUT THAT THING *AWAY*!
BB

STOP *FLASHING* ME!

I HATE HAVING MY PICTURE TAKEN!

Automation is one of those things where, when it doesn't work, it *really* doesn't work.

LARGE PRINT

LIBRARY TIP #64: DON'T COUNT YOUR BOOKS BEFORE THEY'RE SHELVED

I'M GOING TO BE A LIBRARIAN!
SON, PLEASE, NOT AGAIN

THIS PLACE IS AWESOME!
KEEP THIS UP, WE'RE GOING BACK TO THE DEPROGRAMMER.

YOU CAN'T GET THESE FROM READING!
LOOK AT ALL THE BOOKS!
BB

WE ALSO USE TECHNOLOGY IN THE LIBRARY.
SHOULD THIS SOUND LIKE MY BLENDER?
ZBRZBRZBRZBRZBRZBRZBRZBRZBRZBRZ
WHACK!
MMMMMMMMMMMMMMMMMMMM
YOU'RE A NATURAL.

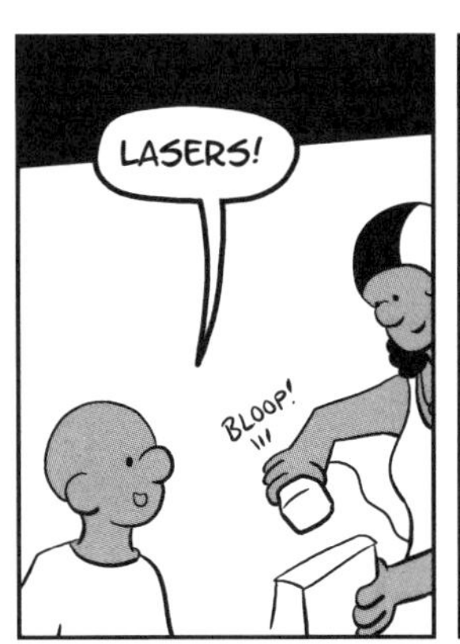
LASERS!
BLOOP!

THE READER'S GUIDE!

COUNTRY LIVING!
STAFF
LEARN TO LIVE WITH IT. HE'S GOING TO BE A LIBRARIAN.
I'LL FIND YOU A SUPPORT GROUP.
BB

LARGE PRINT

THAT'S NOT A WORK SHIRT.
I DISAGREE.

IT'S NOT DRESSY ENOUGH.
IT'S A NICE SHIRT. I SUGGEST YOU QUIT WHILE YOU'RE AHEAD.

WEAR SOMETHING WITH BUTTONS AND A COLLAR TOMORROW.
YOU CAN'T SAY I DIDN'T FORESHADOW YOU.

I'M WRITING YOU UP.
FOR DOING EXACTLY WHAT YOU SAID?

THAT'S NOT *DRESSY*!
IT IS ACCORDING TO YESTERDAY–YOU.

TOMORROW WEAR A ***NORMAL*** DRESS SHIRT WITH A ***NORMAL*** COLLAR AND BUTTONS AND ***NORMAL*** SLEEVES! ***NORMAL***!
USUALLY YOU CATCH ON FASTER THAN THIS.
BB

UNACCEPTABLE!
BE GLAD I DIDN'T SCREEN PRINT YOUR FACE. FULL COLOR IS ***PRICEY!***
MY BOSS
MADE ME
EAR THIS
SHIRT
AN ***INVOICE?*** WE'RE NOT PAYING FOR ***CLOTHES!***
"UNIFORM". AND THE LAW SAYS YOU ***ARE.***
THIS IS GOING TO END WITH YOU BACK IN YOUR FAVORITE T–SHIRT, ISN'T IT?
IT ALWAYS WAS.
BB

YOU CAN'T DO THAT.
CLEANLINESS IS NEXT TO GODLINESS!

WASHING HANDS HELPS PREVENT THE FLU.
YOUR *HANDS* AREN'T THE PROBLEM.
BB

WOULD YOU BELIEVE IT'S A CAT-SHAPED WASHCLOTH?
WOULD YOU BELIEVE WE HAVE A POLICY ABOUT THAT TOO?

I'D LIKE TO DONATE MONEY TO THE LIBRARY!
WONDERFUL!
MROWWWW!

WHAT'S -- ?
DON'T LOOK. JUST PLEASE DON'T LOOK.

WAS THAT A *CAT*?
I DIDN'T SEE ANYTHING.
IS THIS *SOAP*?
JUST WRITE THE CHECK.
BB

THE TRAIL IS FRESH!
KITTY!

THE PROBLEM, AS WE'VE ALREADY EXPERIENCED, IS THAT A *SOAPY* CAT IS A *SLIPPERY* CAT.
HERE, KITTY!

THAT'S NOT REALLY HELPING.
HERE, KITTY KITTY!
BB

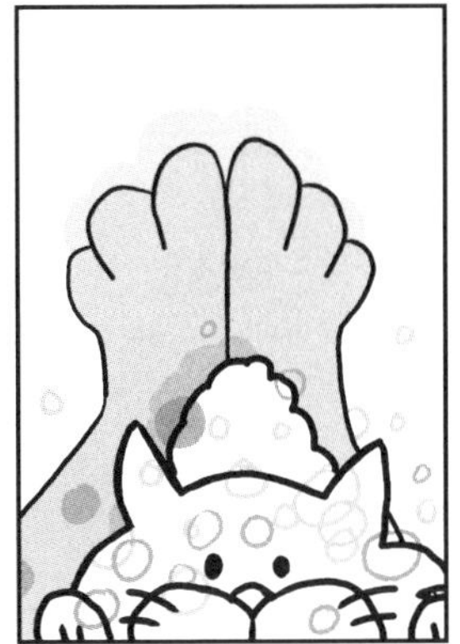

MY NEW FRIEND HAS SHARP CLAWS!
KEEP MOVING TOWARDS THE DOOR.
REH

BUT THERE WASN'T A SIGN!
DEWEY, PUT A NO CAT BATHING SIGN IN THE RESTROOM.

BEFORE OR AFTER I CHARGE HER FOR THESE RUINED BOOKS?
I DIDN'T CHECK THOSE OUT! I'M LEAVING!

GOOD RIDDANCE.
I NEED TO INVITE HER TO RETURN WITHOUT HER CAT!

I'M NOW GOING TO HOLD THIS WOMAN RESPONSIBLE FOR HER OBNOXIOUS BEHAVIOR.

MY DOING SO WILL PROBABLY MAKE MANY OF YOU AS HAPPY AS IT MAKES ME.

BUT PLEASE, HOLD YOUR APPLAUSE UNTIL THE END OF THE CONVERSATION.
BB

I WANT YOU TO PUT THAT IN WRITING.
NO NEED TO KILL A TREE.

SPEAK INTO THIS RECORDER.
I'M FEELING A LITTLE HOARSE.

INSULT ME IN FRONT OF WITNESSES. I DARE YOU.
I PREFER TO MAINTAIN PLAUSIBLE DENIABILITY.
BB

THIS MAN SAYS YOU TOLD HIM WHERE TO GO.
TO BE FAIR, HE ASKED FOR DIRECTIONS.
BB

INSTEAD OF ESCALATING THE SITUATION TRY FINDING A WAY TO CALM THINGS DOWN.
BEFORE I ASK YOU TO LEAVE AGAIN HERE'S A DELICIOUS LOLLYPOP.
I DON'T LIKE GREEN! I WANT RED!
BB

HAVEN'T YOU EVER HEARD OF THE GOLDEN RULE?
I LIVE IT EVERY DAY.

HOW CAN YOU SAY THAT? YOU'RE SO RUDE!
I'M DIRECT. AND I ENJOY DIRECTNESS IN OTHERS.

BUT YOU'RE NOT NICE!
THAT'S A DIFFERENT RULE.

HOW COME NO ONE SHOWED ME THIS PART OF THE LIBRARY BEFORE?
YOU WEREN'T QUALIFIED.

BUT AFTER A CAREFUL ANALYSIS OF BORROWING PATTERNS, CROSS-REFERENCED WITH DEMOGRAPHIC DATA AND YOUR LONG-RUNNING STREAK OF RETURNING BOOKS BEFORE THEIR DUE DATES, WE DECIDED YOU'D EARNED THE PRIVILEGE.

REALLY?
NO. YOU JUST NEVER ASKED.
BB

THERE'S A RUMOR THAT OUR LIBRARY KEEPS ALL OF ITS GOOD BOOKS HIDDEN IN A SECRET ROOM.

SPECIFICALLY, THEY KEEP ASKING FOR A "SHANGRI LA ROOM."

WHAT ELSE HAVE YOU BEEN TELLING THEM?
I'M WEARING THE SACRED HEAD COVERING! AM I WORTHY NOW?
BB

We do a lot of keynotes at book and library conferences. We've been on the receiving end of a number of... *creative* introductions.

"HOW WOULD YOU LIKE TO BE INTRODUCED?"

I FOUND THIS IN MY BOOK.
IT LOOKS LIKE A FORTUNE.

IT IS!
"YOUR DAY IS ABOUT TO GET BETTER."

ISN'T IT MYSTERIOUS?
I HOPE IT'S MEANT FOR ME.
BB

"YOU WILL TAKE AN UNEXPECTED JOURNEY."
I'M TAKING A TRIP LATER TODAY!

THEN IT'S NOT "UNEXPECTED".
I JUST FOUND OUT! I CAME BY TO GET A GUIDE BOOK, AND FOUND THAT!

I'M UNDERWHELMED BY THE COINCIDENCE.
WHAT LOTTERY NUMBER SHOULD I PICK?

"YOU WILL MEET A YOUNG MAN WITH GREAT PROMISE."
I THINK IT'S TALKING ABOUT YOU!

MY PROMISES ARE MORE LIKE THREATS.
EDGY! I LIKE THAT!

I'M OFF.
TO FACE DANGER? BATTLE INSURMOUNTABLE ODDS?

This single comic strip contains an entire standardized test's worth of vocabulary. You may qualify for course credit just by reading it.

Unshelved would be a better strip if we started off with more establishing shots.

LARGE PRINT

I PAID HIM OUT OF MY OWN POCKET.
I NEEDED A DOLLAR'S WORTH OF PEACE AND QUIET.

YOU TELL US TO DO ANYTHING THAT DE-ESCALATES ANGRY PATRONS.

I NEVER EXPECTED **CASH** TO BE INVOLVED.
THEN I WON'T TELL YOU ABOUT THE **FOOT MASSAGES**.
BB

I HEAR IF WE MAKE TROUBLE WE MIGHT TAKE HOME SOME CASH!
NOT TRUE.
BB

SHOULD I START BEHAVING BADLY NOW?
ONLY IF YOU WANT TO LEAVE THE BUILDING.

I STILL SMELL AN OPPORTUNITY HERE.
THAT'S NOT AN OPPORTUNITY. THAT'S A PROBLEM.

DOES YOUR SCANNER WORK BECAUSE OF THE **WAVE** NATURE OF LIGHT OR THE **PARTICLE** NATURE OF LIGHT?
NOT A CLUE!

DON'T YOU **UNDERSTAND** THE TECHNOLOGY YOU USE?
IT GOES "BEEP"!

HOW DOES IT FEEL TO BE **IGNORANT**?
SURPRISINGLY BLISSFUL!

We literally cannot make up stuff that hasn't happened to someone somewhere. You wouldn't believe how many carpet-vertigo stories we've now heard.

LARGE PRINT

I'VE NAILED DOWN FUNDING FOR OUR NEW CARPET.
NO NEED.

IT'S GOING TO MEAN MORE BUDGET CUTS.
I'VE AGREED TO HELP THE ONE PATRON WITH THE ISSUE.

WE NEED TO THINK *BIGGER*!
MAYBE WE JUST NEED TO *THINK*.

I NEED A POWER CORD FOR MY VIC-20.
WHY DO YOU THINK *WE'D* HAVE ONE?

I WAS HOPING YOU'D HAVE A SPARE IN YOUR *ARCHIVE OF FORGOTTEN TECHNOLOGY*.
WE DON'T HAVE SUCH A THING.
BB

WHAT DO YOU CALL *THOSE*?
OUR PUBLIC ACCESS PCs?
OKAY, POINT TAKEN. I'LL CHECK IN THE BACK.

WHO'S IN CHARGE?
RIGHT NOW? ME.

I DEMAND -
JUST TO BE CLEAR, THAT DOESN'T MEAN MUCH.

FOR WHOM SHOULD I SAVE MY *ENERGY*?
MY MANAGER. SHE'S SLIGHTLY LESS POWERLESS.
BB

MY BOOKMARK WAS RIGHT HERE, PAGE 275.

IT'S NOT THERE NOW.
THAT'S WHY I'M COMPLAINING!

WHY DO YOU NEED A BOOKMARK IF YOU KNOW --
DON'T GET RATIONAL WITH ME, YOUNG MAN!

WHY DID YOU RETURN A BOOK WITH YOUR BOOKMARK IN IT?
IT WAS DUE.

WHY DIDN'T YOU REMOVE YOUR BOOKMARK?
I HADN'T FINISHED THE BOOK YET.

WHY DID YOU THINK IT WOULD STAY THERE?
WHY WOULDN'T IT?
BB

I CHECKED THE LOST AND FOUND. NO BOOKMARKS.
BOTTOM OF THE BOOKDROP?

NOT THERE, EITHER.
MAYBE AN ERRANT BREEZE DEPOSITED IT INTO ANOTHER BOOK.

... HOW EXACTLY WOULD WE FIND THAT?
YOU START ON THE LEFT END OF THE STACKS, I'LL START ON THE RIGHT.
BB

GOT A PIECE OF PAPER?

I LIKE SIMPLE BOOKMARKS TOO.
I MISPLACED THE TOENAIL CLIPPING I NORMALLY USE.
BB

DISSUE!
HERE.

LEGGO!
THE ONE STICKING OUT THE TOP? THAT'S FOR YOU.

YOU UNDERESTIMATE MY MUCUS MEMBRANES!
YOU OVERESTIMATE OUR TISSUE BUDGET.
BB

TAKE WHAT YOU NEED.
I NEED THE WHOLE BOX!

I'LL REPHRASE: HELP YOURSELF TO **SEVERAL**.
THAT'S A VERY FLUID TERM.

PLEASE KEEP YOUR FLUIDS TO YOURSELF.
I'M **TRYING**!

MY HAND IS **STUCK**!
YOU TRIED TO GRAB THEM **ALL**.

LET GO SO THAT I CAN GET MY HAND FREE.
I'M NOT LETTING GO.

IT'S NOT LIKE I ASKED FOR THE **HAND SANITIZER**!
YOU STILL HAVE SANITIZER? I'LL TAKE **TWO**!

THERE'S A LINE AROUND THE BLOCK FOR OUR COMPUTERS.
LOOKS LIKE WORD FINALLY GOT OUT ABOUT OUR SERVICES!
WHAT BRINGS YOU TO THE LIBRARY ON THIS CRISP WINTER DAY?
I'VE GOT TO FILE FOR UNEMPLOYMENT SO THAT I CAN EAT.
BB

YOU APPLIED FOR **THREE** JOBS LAST WEEK!
I DIDN'T EVEN GET AN **INTERVIEW**.
BB

I'M SURE NEXT WEEK WILL BE **BETTER**!
COULDN'T BE **WORSE**.

LOOK ON THE **BRIGHT** SIDE...
EXCUSE ME, MISS **STABLE GOVERNMENT JOB**. THE **SUNNY APPROACH** ISN'T CHEERING ME UP.

I NEED THAT BOOK TO PREPARE FOR MY JOB INTERVIEW MONDAY!
THERE'S A FOUR MONTH WAIT.

WE HAVE A GREAT REFERENCE BOOK ON WORLD WAR II...
IF I DON'T KILL YOU, I'LL USE IT DURING JOB INTERVIEWS AS AN EXAMPLE OF HOW WELL I HANDLE STRESS!
BB

SNIFF SNIFF

SOMETHING'S ROTTEN IN THE STATE OF DENMARK!
SHAKESPEARE IN THE PARK FLASHBACK?

SOMETHING **STINKS** IN HERE.
NOW YOU'VE GONE COLLOQUIAL.
BB

PEOPLE ARE COMPLAINING ABOUT A **SMELL**.
THEY'RE ALWAYS COMPLAINING ABOUT SOMETHING.

FIND IT.
I'M NOT A ***BLOODHOUND***.

AFRAID OF WHAT YOU MIGHT UNCOVER?
YES. AND EVEN MORE AFRAID I'LL HAVE TO CLEAN IT UP.
BB

THAT **SMELL** MEANS THE LIBRARY ISN'T CLEAN!
THE FACT THAT IT'S A ***LIBRARY*** MEANS THE LIBRARY ISN'T CLEAN.

THE SMELL IS JUST A ***WARNING***. THE REST OF THE CONTAMINATION IS SILENT AND INVISIBLE.

TAMARA'S AT THE SINK AGAIN?
THREE MONTHS OF SOAP IN ONE DAY.
BB

TODAY'S PROGRAM
"LIBRARY DETECTIVE"
1. WHAT IS THAT SMELL?
2. WHERE IS IT COMING FROM?
CROWDSOURCING!
BB

I KNOW WHAT'S MAKING THE SMELL.
I DON'T WANT TO KNOW.

IT'S NOT MY FAULT THIS TIME.
I REALLY JUST DON'T WANT TO KNOW.
HOW MUCH TO MAKE IT GO AWAY?

YOU CAUGHT ME OFF GUARD. I DON'T HAVE A PRICE SHEET PREPARED.
I'LL PAY DOUBLE IF YOU NEVER SPEAK OF IT AGAIN.

IT SMELLS MUCH BETTER OUT HERE!
THANK MERV.

THANKS. I THINK.
I'VE NEVER SEEN SUCH A BIG
IN RETURN I'M HOSTING A HALO 3 LAN PARTY FOR MERV AND HIS FRIENDS.

YOU CAN'T DO THAT HERE!
EXACTLY. SEE YOU TOMORROW.
OR THE NEXT DAY.
BB

THAT WAS THE UNION REP. HE'S AFRAID WE'RE WORKING OUTSIDE OUR JOB DESCRIPTIONS.

YOU TOLD ME MY JOB WAS "MAKING PEOPLE HAPPY".
IT IS. STARTING WITH THE UNION REP.

MY GILA MONSTER HAS A FROG LEG STUCK IN ITS THROAT.
WHOSE JOB IS IT TO MAKE **HIM** HAPPY?
BB

YOU'RE NOT ALLOWED TO SHELVE BOOKS.

BUDDY DOES THAT.

YOU TAKE THEM **OFF** THE SHELF.
WEIRD. I'M USUALLY **HAPPY** WHEN YOU ASK ME TO WORK LESS.
BB

I CHECKED. BUDDY'S IN FAVOR OF ME RESHELVING AN OCCASIONAL BOOK.
IT'S NOT YOUR DUTY.
READ

WHERE ARE THE COMPUTER BOOKS?
DON'T ANSWER! YOU'RE NOT QUALIFIED!
BB

WELL? TELL HIM!
I NEED TO CHECK MY JOB DESCRIPTION.
CAN ONE OF YOU PLEASE JUST **POINT**?

LARGE PRINT

WOULD YOU MIND PICKING THAT UP?
NOT AT ALL!

WHERE ARE YOU GOING?
I NEED TO MAKE SURE I'M ALLOWED TO DO THAT.

GOOD NEWS MA'AM!
MA'AM?

YOU'RE NOT SUPPOSED TO RESHELVE THAT.

PUT THE BOOK BACK ON THE TABLE AND RAISE YOUR HANDS.

NOW BACK AWAY SLOWLY.
YOU KNOW WHAT PEOPLE APPRECIATE? STRUCTURE!
BB

DON'T YOU KNOW THAT THE FLU **FEEDS** ON SUGAR?
THEN I'D BETTER EAT **MORE** TO KEEP IT **HAPPY**.
BB

FURTHERMORE --
THERE'S A FURTHERMORE? HOLD ON A SECOND.

YOU'RE TAKING **NOTES**?
YOUR IRRITATION IS UNUSUALLY COMPLEX.

AAARRRGGGGHHH!
HOW MANY G'S DOES THAT HAVE?
BB

DONE COMPLAINING?
I'M NOT GOING TO BECOME A DINNER PARTY ANECDOTE.

I DON'T NEED NOTES FOR THAT. I JUST MAKE UP THE DETAILS.

THOUGH IN YOUR CASE, I WON'T NEED TO DO ANY EXAGGERATING.
AH, LOOKS LIKE YOU'RE READY TO CONTINUE.

ARE YOU LISTENING TO **ANYTHING** I'M SAYING??
IT WOULD BE HARD **NOT** TO HEAR YOU.

THEN **LOOK** AT ME!
CAN'T. NEED TO GET THIS DOWN.

WHY?
YOU HAVE SERIOUS LONG-TERM PROBLEM POTENTIAL. I'M ARCHIVING YOUR INITIAL RANT FOR FUTURE GENERATIONS.
BB

Watch out, Dewey. That stuff is *addictive*.

WE'RE FIELD TESTING LIBRARY MATERIALS DISPENSERS.
SANJAY, GO FIND THE CHEAT CODES FOR THIS THING.

HOW DO YOU LIKE OUR MEDIA DISPENSER?
IT LOOKS LIKE AN OLD VENDING MACHINE.

IT'S BEEN ADAPTED FOR LIBRARY MATERIALS.
NOT EVERYONE GOT THAT MEMO.

I NEED A MARS BAR!
LOOK! THE NEW BRUCE WILLIS MOVIE!

IT CHECKS OUT BOOKS! IT CHECKS IN BOOKS! IT'S IDIOT PROOF!

DO YOU THINK IT'S ADJUSTABLE?
I HOPE NOT.

I THINK I FEEL A DVD SET.
BETTER NOT BE ANOTHER AUDIOBOOK.

MY HAND IS STUCK!
RELAX. JIGGLE IT. BUT DON'T LET GO.

HAVING FUN?
WE'RE TRYING, BUT YOUR MACHINE ISN'T COOPERATING.
I THINK YOU NEED CLEARER WARNING STICKERS.
BB

THERE'S JUST A SINGLE BUTTON. HOW DO I KNOW WHAT I'M GETTING?

YOU'LL FIND OUT WHEN IT COMES OUT THE SLOT. IT'S LIKE CHRISTMAS!

I DON'T WANT THIS BOOK.
IT'S EXACTLY LIKE CHRISTMAS.
BB

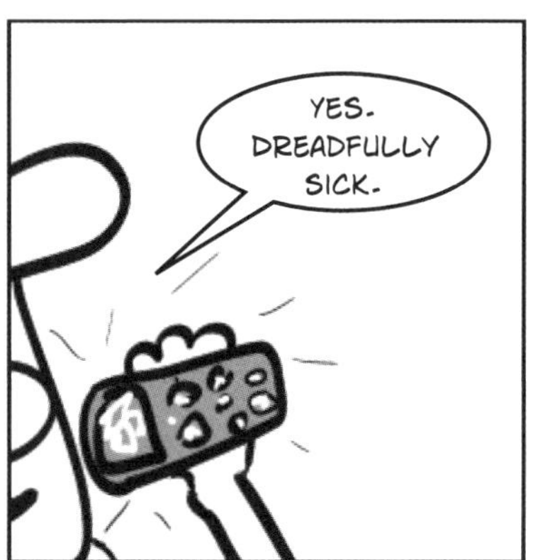

Every year on Bill's birthday Gene draws a strip Bill writes. It's always... interesting.

THE NEW BOOKLISTS ARE OUT! I'M ABUZZ WITH WHAT WAS INCLUDED!
AND EXCLUDED!

LIBRARIANS WORKED HARD TO MAKE THOSE LISTS!
NOW I KNOW WHY I'M NEVER INVITED.
LOOK AT THIS ONE.

"BOOKS TEEN BOYS WOULD READ (IF THEY KNEW THEY EXISTED)"
IS IT NEW?
VERY. I JUST WROTE IT.
BB

YOU CAN'T MAKE YOUR OWN BOOKLIST!
READERS ADVISORY IS A BIG PART OF MY JOB.

THIS BOOK CONTAINS ADULT CONTENT!
DON'T FORGET THE GRAPHIC VIOLENCE!

WE CAN'T BE RESPONSIBLE FOR KIDS READING THESE BOOKS!
EXACTLY. ONLY THEIR PARENTS CAN BE RESPONSIBLE FOR THEM.
BB

YOU GAVE MY SON THIS BOOK!
NEVER SEEN HIM BEFORE IN MY LIFE.

THEN YOU GAVE HIM THIS LIST OF SMUT!
NO. BUT I DID MAKE IT BROADLY AVAILABLE.

WELL, HE READ SOMETHING FROM IT! I HOPE YOU'RE ALL HAPPY!
HOW SWEET! WE HOPE YOU'RE HAPPY TOO!
BB

I'M GOING TO SPEND THE NEXT MONTH ANSWERING COMPLAINT LETTERS ABOUT YOUR BOOKLIST!

LET THE RECORD SHOW THAT I PROMOTE READING AND WRITING.
BB

Seldom has a strip prompted such a response from librarians. We were inundated with stories and photos featuring prominent, but tragically ignored, tax form signage.

YOU'RE OUT OF THE TAX FORM I NEED.
SORRY TO HEAR THAT.

WHAT ARE YOU GOING TO DO FOR ME?
I CAN ORDER A COPY FROM THE IRS.
SHOULD BE HERE IN 6 WEEKS.

USELESS!
OR, IF YOU'RE PATIENT AND POLITE, I CAN PRINT A COPY RIGHT NOW.
BB

CAN YOU HELP ME?
LOOKS LIKE YOU'RE DOING EVERYTHING RIGHT.

IT'S NOT DOING WHAT I WANT!
I DON'T HAVE ANY BETTER IDEAS.

TAKE OVER. I WANT SOMEONE TO BLAME.
SURE. IT'S ONE OF MY PRIMARY JOB RESPONSIBILITIES.
BB

CAN I USE THE PHONE?
IS IT FOR A RIDE HOME?

I COULD SAY THAT. BUT WE BOTH KNOW I'D BE LYING.
IT'S PART OF THE DANCE WE MUST DANCE.

IT'S FOR A RIDE HOME.
TOMORROW WE'LL PRACTICE PIROUETTES.
BB

DID YOU KNOW THE WORD "GULLIBLE" ISN'T IN *WIKIPEDIA*?
IT ISN'T? I'LL PUT IT IN RIGHT NOW!
BB

THAT JOKE DIDN'T UPDATE WELL.
SOMEONE BEAT ME TO IT!

YOU'RE READING SO WELL!
I'M AFRAID I HAVE SOME BAD NEWS.

YOU'RE CLOSING EARLY?
NO. I NEED YOU TO LOWER YOUR VOICE.

I'M PRACTICALLY WHISPERING!
THAT'S WHAT I WAS AFRAID OF.
BB

YOUR VOICE CARRIES QUITE A DISTANCE.
HOW FAR AWAY CAN YOU HEAR ME?

ACROSS THE LIBRARY. INTO THE STAFF ROOM.
WHAT WERE WE TALKING ABOUT?

BRUSSELS SPROUTS.
OKAY.
THEY MAKE HER FART.
I BELIEVE YOU!
BB

I'M TRYING TO BE QUIET!
I DON'T THINK IT'S POSSIBLE.

YOU MAKE IT SOUND LIKE I'M SHRIEKING.
I'D SAY YOUR VOICE HAS... UNIQUE QUALITIES.

"TEACH YOURSELF SIGN LANGUAGE IN 21 DAYS."
SEE YOU IN THREE WEEKS!
BB

Every year on Gene's birthday Bill agrees to draw a strip featuring bathroom humor.

A rarity - this *Unshelved* strip doesn't feature any of our regular characters.

LARGE PRINT

YOU ONLY HAVE THE FIRST BOOK IN THIS SERIES.
I'LL TAKE YOUR WORD FOR IT.

NOT JUST HERE. THE ENTIRE SYSTEM!
CLEARLY YOU KNOW HOW TO USE THE ONLINE CATALOG.

BUT THE SEQUELS ARE ALREADY OUT!
SO IS OUR BOOK-BUYING BUDGET.

YOU HAVE TO BUY THE OTHER TWO BOOKS IN THIS SERIES!
WE'D LIKE TO BUT WE DON'T HAVE THE MONEY.

BUT YOU GOT ME HOOKED!
LET ME FIND ANOTHER BOOK YOU'D ENJOY.

IF I ASKED FOR CAKE DO YOU THINK I'D WANT A MUFFIN?
NO, BUT I THINK YOU'D EAT ONE IF YOU WERE HUNGRY.
BB

YOU'RE CORRUPT. YOU RUIN OUR HOPES.
OUR DREAMS!
WELL AT LEAST YOU'RE NOT BEING DRAMATIC ABOUT IT.
BB

I'LL PUT IN A REQUEST TO BUY THE SEQUELS NEXT YEAR.
I AM NOT A PATIENT WOMAN!

YOU COULD GO TO A BOOKSTORE.
AND WASTE MY MONEY ON THIS JUNK?

Bill says: the first panel of this strip may be the funniest thing Gene has ever written.

IF I GET A CARD NOW, YOU'LL REMEMBER WHO I AM.
TRUE. YOU MADE A SCENE. NOW YOU'RE MEMORABLE.

TRY LAYING LOW FOR A FEW MONTHS. THEN COME IN AND GET A CARD WHEN I'M NOT HERE.

THAT'S SUSPICIOUSLY WELL THOUGHT OUT.
YOU'RE NOT OUR ONLY PARANOID.
I'M PREPARING TO ENTER THE LIBRARY. EVERYBODY CLOSE YOUR EYES!
BB

Our tribute to *Evil, Inc.'s* Brad Guigar on his tenth anniversary in cartooning. That's him, laughing at his own jokes as always.

LIBRARY TIP #69: IT'S NOT ALL ABOUT YOU
WHY DO YOU HATE ME SO MUCH?
IT'S MORE OF AN ALL-PURPOSE DISRESPECT.
BB

LIBRARY TIP #70: WINNERS NEVER QUIT
I FINISHED MY SUMMER READING GOAL!
SUMMER ENDED MONTHS AGO.
NO MORE PRIZES?
YOU'RE A LITTLE OLD FOR "THE POUT," AREN'T YOU?
JUST FIND ME A PRIZE SO I CAN GET MY PARENTS OFF MY BACK.
HERE'S A PENCIL. IT SAYS "I'M A PRINCESS."

LIBRARY TIP #71: QUITTERS NEVER WIN
I WILL FIND THE INFORMATION FOR THAT WOMAN.
SHE LEFT HALF AN HOUR AGO.
NO ONE VALUES PERSEVERANCE ANY MORE.
SERIOUSLY. YOU CAN STOP LOOKING.
NO. I CAN'T.
BB

NO COMPLAINTS ABOUT THOSE KIDS?
A FEW SILENT PLEAS, BUT I'VE IGNORED THEM.

THEY'RE BLOCKING THE DOOR!
YOU CAN GET PAST IF YOU TRY. TAKES A BIT OF MANEUVERING.

YOU'RE MAKING THIS MY PROBLEM, AREN'T YOU?
OH LOOK, IT'S MY BREAK.

THIS IS A FREE COUNTRY.
AND PEOPLE NEED TO BE **FREE** TO COME INSIDE.

YOU'RE FREE TO **MOVE** OR TO **LEAVE**.
THEY'RE FREE TO **TRY**.
AND **YOU'RE** FREE TO **MAKE** US.

HOW MUCH DOES IT COST TO CHECK OUT THIS BOOK?
IT'S FREE!
BB

ARE THEY GONE YET?
THEY'RE ON THEIR WAY OUT.
HI, I NEED A SQUAD CAR AT THE LIBRARY.
A BUNCH OF TEENAGERS LOITERING BY THE FRONT DOOR.
THEY WON'T LET ANYONE IN.
FIVE OF THEM.
YEAH, PRETTY BIG.
BB

WE'RE ON OUR OWN.
THE TALL ONE JUST ATE THE PAY PHONE.

For April Fools 2010, a bunch of comic strips featured no text. This was our contribution.

About the closest we get to cutting-edge technology humor.
This may explain why Bill started a second comic strip.

I SHALL BE CONSTANTLY VIGILANT ABOUT MY PRIVACY.
I'M THROUGH RESPONDING TO SPAM AND POSTING TO SOCIAL NETWORKING SITES.
I WILL BEWARE EAVESDROPPERS, SHUN SURVEILLANCE CAMERAS, AND SOW CONFUSION SO THAT DATA MINERS CAN'T FOLLOW MY TRACKS.
I SHALL STEEP MYSELF IN ANONYMITY!
I WILL NO LONGER GOSSIP.

YOU DROPPED THIS.
THANKS! HOW ELSE WOULD I REMEMBER ALL MY PASSWORDS?

SEND OUT MY SON!
SORRY, I'M NOT A PAGING SERVICE.

I'M OUTSIDE IN MY CAR. I CAN SEE HIM SITTING RIGHT THERE!
STILL NOT MY JOB.

I'LL HAVE YOU FIRED!
I DOUBT IT. YOU'D NEED TO LEAVE YOUR CAR.
BB

THERE ARE NO LEAVES ON THE TREES!
IT'S CALLED WINTER.

THE KIDS AREN'T IN SCHOOLS!
IT'S CALLED A WEEKEND.

THE LITTLE BEIGE MEN WON'T LEAVE ME ALONE.
I'M CALLING FOR HELP.

CONFERENCE TIP: RESIST PEER PRESSURE

CONFERENCE TIP: TELL THEM WANT THEY WANT TO HEAR

CONFERENCE TIP: THERE'S NO SUCH THING AS A FREE BUFFET

CONFERENCE TIP: TAKE YOUR TIME
WE'RE LATE!
NO ONE IS TAKING ATTENDANCE.
I DON'T WANT TO MISS THE BEGINNING!
AND I DON'T WANT TO STAY UNTIL THE END.
TWO SEATS IN THE FRONT ROW!
I'LL BE CROUCHED BACK HERE, PLAYING MY DS.

CONFERENCE TIP: BE YOURSELF
YOU DON'T LOOK LIKE THE DIRECTOR OF A LARGE LIBRARY SYSTEM.
HEAD OF COLLECTION DEVELOPMENT?
"BOOKCART TESTER"?
WHERE ARE THE SADDLES?

CONFERENCE TIP: DON'T BE A TWIT
BLOGGING?
LIVE TWEETING!
THE SPEAKER'S ARGUMENTS ARE PRETTY INVOLVED...
I'M PARAPHRASING!
"MORE BLAH BLAH."
"SOME DOOFUS SAT DOWN NEXT TO ME."
IT'S FOR POSTERITY!

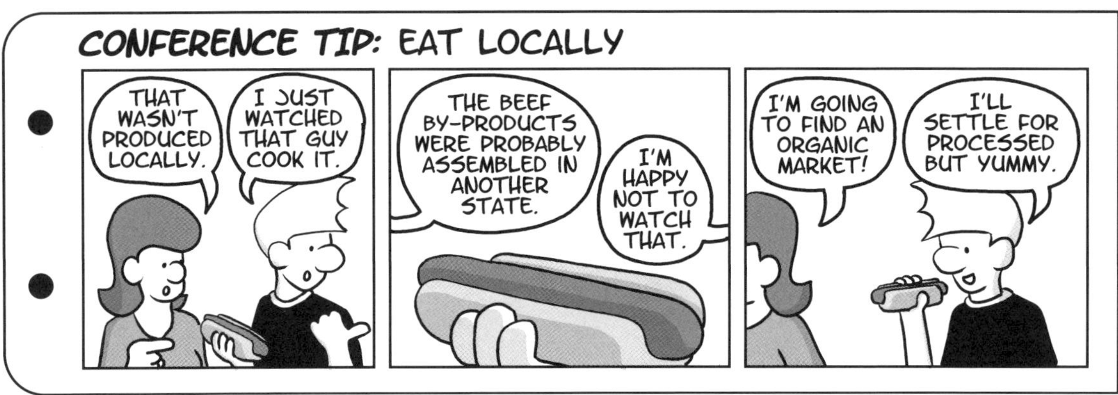

Bill was pretty happy with his drawing of that hot dog.

I'M LOOKING FOR THIS BOOK.
NEVER HEARD OF IT AND IT'S NOT IN THE CATALOG.

IT WAS PUBLISHED *TODAY*.
AND YOU THOUGHT WE MIGHT HAVE IT ALREADY?

WHY *WOULDN'T* YOU?
I'LL CHECK TO SEE IF WE HAVE AN UNPOPULAR BOOK BY THE SAME AUTHOR.

YOU *BUY* THE BOOK. YOU PUT IT ON THE *SHELVES*.
IT'S NOT THAT EASY.

WE HAVE TO ADD IT TO OUR CATALOG FIRST, SO THAT YOU CAN SEE THAT IT'S NOT HERE YET.
THEN WE OBSCURE THE COVER WITH LABELS.
THEN WE COAT IT WITH MYLAR TO PROTECT IT FROM YOUR GRUBBY HANDS.

HOW LONG DOES IT *TAKE*?
LONG ENOUGH TO BUILD UP A DAUNTING WAITING LIST!
BB

EVEN WITH ALL OF YOUR PROCESSING, IT SHOULDN'T TAKE LONG TO GET A NEW BOOK ON THE SHELF!
TRUE. IF IT WERE JUST *ONE* BOOK.
BUT WE'RE TALKING *THOUSANDS* OF BOOKS. *TENS* OF THOUSANDS.
IT CREATES QUITE A BACKLOG!
BB

LOOK! THE 2007 ALMANAC ARRIVED!
I'LL HEAD OVER TO THE BOOKSTORE.

This page intentionally left mostly blank.